The Ultimate Guide on How to Become A Internet Marketing Guru Fast

by Neo Monefa

Table of Contents

1. What Is Internet Marketing?

If you are starting out a business with a lot of players in the industry, it is essential that you are technologically updated and advanced in order to keep up with the competition. While you may not have resources to compete head on with the other players, technology at least levels the playing field. This is where inbound marketing comes in.

Internet marketing is a means of promoting your business through various content marketing platforms like social media, blogs, videos, e-books, white papers, podcasts, and search engine optimization (SEO) tools. You create interesting content about your business that is distributed through these platforms. It aims to make your company more accessible and to bring your customers closer to your brand.

In contrast, traditional outbound marketing refers to media advertisements, direct mailers, fliers, and telemarketing calls, to name a few. Inbound marketing is preferred over outbound marketing because it is not as hard sell as the latter. It does not annoy customers as much as outbound marketing normally does.

With internet marketing, you create content that will specifically appeal to your target market. You want them to be aware of your brand and hopefully, they will be interested in what you have to offer. You use a personalized approach to make sure that your content is responsive to the needs of your individual customers. To maximize the content that you have created, you must make it available through different channels where your customers can access them.

Once you have your target market's attention, you would want to convert these visitors to leads and eventually into sales. You want them to be repeat customers as well.

You should analyze the data you gather from inbound marketing, as these are highly valuable. They tell you where to find the right customers and what your customers want, among others.

The Importance of Content Marketing

With a lot of marketing tools available, you might ask why content marketing is important. Primarily, it is a powerful tool for promoting your brand, making your company easier to find. Apart from this, here are other reasons why content marketing is important:

• People will not be suspicious of your motives and they will be more trusting because it does not appear as if you are selling something. As mentioned above, it is not as hard sell as other traditional types of marketing so people would not see you as someone pushy.
• Your content is relevant to your target market so they will find it informative, interesting, entertaining, enlightening, and even helpful. This will encourage them to share the content with people within their circles, giving your content a wider reach. After all, word of mouth is still one of the best marketing tools that your business can have.

• The more relevant your content is, the more engaged your customers would be. They will spend more time reading your content and learning about your business. Hopefully, this would be converted into increased interest in your company.

• Updated and high quality content will help your company's search rankings. Search engines prefer content that are viral and are often shared in social circles. The way search engines view your content is highly important because it dictates where your content lands in their results pages.

• The more people who have access to your content, the more leads that you have which could also translate to higher sales.

• The types of content you can create are limitless. You can create content that are relevant to different types of customers that you have. You can ask other writers to create them for you. You can even use materials created by your own customers. For instance, if your clients create reviews or testimonials about your business, you can incorporate these in the content that you distribute through social media. This would make your marketing tools more credible and trustworthy.

These are just some of the reasons why content marketing is important for your business. As you go along the way and as we progress through this book, you will find even more reasons why inbound marketing should be a priority for your company.

The Method of Re-purposing Content for Being Seen Everywhere

How can you take one piece of main content and turn it into an entire campaign?

Understandably, if you are just starting out with your business, you will not have overflowing resources which would enable you to create a lot of content. Thus, it is important that you learn how to create high quality content and to use this efficiently.

Re-purposing your content would allow an efficient use of your resources. Others could view this as recycling of what you already have. But it is not just a matter of re-using or copying. Re-purposing means re-creating or tweaking your content to suit your destination format such as a social media post or a blog entry. This will ensure that the content that reaches your customers also match their preferences.

The basic step in re-purposing your content is the creation of a main article or content that you will use as a template or source for the re-purposed content that you will distribute later on.

To illustrate, imagine that you are starting a personal injury legal practice. You can create one main article every week. For instance, you can make an article on guidelines on what to look for in a personal injury lawyer. Out of this main article, you can create two blog entries, perhaps on fee arrangements with the lawyers and the roles that lawyers play in settling a personal injury claim. You can include videos and images on the blog posts to make them more interesting. Based on these article and blog entries, you can come up with five social media updates. Perhaps you can use an interesting quote from the blog entry as a status update on your social media accounts.

Now that you know what internet marketing is and how important it is for your business, it is now time to master the art of internet marketing. Here are tips on how you can be a marketing guru by spending less than one hour per day.

2. Social Media Marketing for Beginners

For the last several years, social media has been exploding. A decade ago, people were using mostly blogs, MySpace pages, and Geocities pages online, but since then, massive new gateways for communication and interaction have emerged. The big players on the social media scene today are household names like Facebook, Twitter, YouTube, Google Plus, LinkedIn, and Pinterest. Each of these sites has millions of unique visitors each month, and most importantly, these visitors come back repeatedly, often integrating the sites into their daily routines.

It's no surprise, then, that big businesses caught on to the outstanding potential of social media. Social media serves a myriad of functions for businesses of all kinds: market research, public relations, marketing and sales, customer service, and more.

For people who are shy when it comes to social media—or even technology in general—the idea of harnessing the power of social media might be intimidating. Fortunately, this guide will break down the important concepts of social media into bite-sized pieces. You will not only understand what each of these major social media platforms is, but you will also have a clear sense of what each of them can contribute to the success of your business.

Before we get into all the specifics though, let's look at what social media really is. What distinguishes a social media site like Facebook from so-called "traditional media," and why do those distinctions matter?

Put simply, social media is an umbrella term for online communities of people who interact by creating, sharing, exchanging, and conversing. The "social" aspect of social media refers to the fact that everyday people are part of a virtual community. Any website or forum that allows the creation and exchange of user-generated content qualifies as social media.

The "media" aspect of social media refers to the fact that these communities are creating, distributing, and talking about all kinds of content: text, photos, audio, and video. Most people think of "the media" as radio stations, big news networks on television, and print publications like newspapers, but these media outlets no longer have a monopoly on content, nor do they have a stranglehold over whose voice is heard.

How does social media differ from traditional media? Think about it as the difference between a one-way street and a two-way street. In the past, if you wanted to find out what was going on in the world, you checked the newspaper, listened to the radio, or watched your local news channel. These sources of information were mostly one-way: they disseminated information, and you consumed it. There were letters to the editor and chances to call in, but even with these opportunities for dialogue, the media outlets still chose whose voice was heard.

Social media changes all that. It's a two-way street now. As a business owner, you and your customers now have equal footing when it comes to communication. It's up to you to seize the opportunity that represents.

3. How to Write A Valuable Blog Post

The key to starting a successful internet marketing campaign is learning how to create content that your target market will find informative and valuable. As mentioned above, you should start off with a main article or blog post that you can re-purpose for other marketing platforms.

Blogging is not just about coming up with an article about your brand. There are certain tips and tricks you need to follow to make sure that your content is effective. Here are some of them:

Keywords are Key

Since you will be utilizing online technology in marketing your company, it is essential that you know the buzzwords that will make your business easier to find on the Internet. You need to research on what keywords are relevant to your industry or the words that people normally use when they look for businesses like yours online. Knowing the right keywords will not only make your company accessible, it will also narrow down the topics that you can write about in your blog. You can also read up on other SEO techniques to ensure that search engines will look at your blog post favorably.

Ready, Aim, Fire

Before you start writing your blog, you should first know the objective behind your article. For some writers, this means coming up with a conclusion first before starting with the body of the content. This is important to streamline the things that you will write in your blog. It helps you get rid of unnecessary and unrelated topics and allows you to focus on the main idea that you want to convey.

Out with the Outline

Any successful writer will tell you how important it is to prepare an outline before you start writing anything. An outline ensures that your thoughts and ideas are properly arranged to make your blog post easier to read. Half the job is done once you have an outline because all you need to do now is fill in the blanks.

Cut to the Chase

Blame it on the Internet and all these social networking sites, but we have to admit that people have short attention spans nowadays. No one really has the time to read through a lengthy, boring, and irrelevant article. Thus, it is important that you go straight to the point and you catch your audience's attention in the first few lines of your blog post. Otherwise, you might end up losing what could have been potential clients. Be creative and interesting without bluffing and sacrificing the quality of your article.

Informative and Valuable Content

Your clients would want to get something out of your blog entry, otherwise, they will just be wasting their time. Thus, it is your responsibility to come up with content that they will find informative, valuable, and relevant. Here are some ideas to help you do that:

- Use relevant news items related to your industry.
- Talk about the fading and emerging trends in your industry.
- Think of topics that your clients will find engaging.
- Write articles about the big players in your industry.
- Share your opinion about the topics listed above, with solid evidence or sources to back you up.
- Read up on materials relevant to your industry to keep you updated – these can be blogs, newsletters, websites, etc.

Edit, Edit, Edit

A good blog entry is useless if it is full of grammatical errors. You do not want to lose your clients simply because they feel that you cannot compose a grammatically correct content. Start off with your

word processor's spelling and grammar checkers. Afterwards, do something else first then go back to what you wrote. This is important to give you fresh eyes. Read your blog post and make the necessary adjustments to polish your work.

4. Where and How to Distribute A Blog Post for Maximum Exposure

Creating an informative and valuable blog post is not the end. You need to find good places to distribute it for maximum exposure for your brand. Here are some of them:

Social Media

Your number one go-to-place should always be your social media accounts. You have contacts there who are following you primarily because they are interested in what you have to offer. You already have part of their attention, you just need to feed them with good content to keep them engaged.

You can post links to your blog post in your Facebook, Google Plus, and Twitter accounts. Take advantage of the opportunity to interact with your followers. Leave comments that can stir up discussions. Find time to reply to your followers' questions and to address their comments. Follow through is essential to keep them hooked.

Do not limit your options to your own social networking accounts. In Facebook alone, there are likely a number of groups or pages for the industry that you belong to. The people included in these groups or pages are again part of your target market who are most probably interested in reading your blog post. Post a link to your blog in these groups or pages. But do so with caution as some sites treat self-promotion as spam.

E-mail List

Similar to your social networking accounts, your e-mail lists are another good sources of targeted customers for your brand. These lists can include your relatives who are obviously willing to support you. These can also include your friends and other people who work in the same industry.

However, you should also be on the lookout for lists that include potential customers who are only interested to know more about your products. They might just be after what you are selling and they might not really care about your new blog posts. You run the risk of turning them off and they might interpret your e-mail as hard sell marketing. Weigh the risks versus the potential returns for your business.

Perhaps you can try to send to the e-mail list a link to your blog post and include some information on new products or promotions that you may have. If some of the people in your list do not care about your article, at least you can still provide them with relevant content about the items you are offering. If they still react negatively to your e-mail, then maybe you can consider taking them off your mailing list for blog entries and only send them product-related e-mails.

Groups/Communities

Another useful source that you should tap would be groups or communities for your industry. These groups can also refer to the blog groups within your area. Ask them to share the link to your blog post in their respective blogs or groups. These group members have their own followers and supporters who could also be interested in your brand. This could mean a wider reach for the blog entry that you have created.

You might be shy or you might feel awkward about asking these groups or communities to share your blog entry. To avoid this situation, perhaps you can include a reference to their group or blog in your own entry by posting a link. These groups or bloggers would definitely appreciate the special mention that you gave them so they would be willing to share your blog entry as well.

Another technique would be to offer the same help to them in the future. You can ask a fellow blogger to share your entry in his blog and let him know that if he has an entry that would be relevant to your target market, you can also share the same in your blog. Of course, try to limit the use of this means to avoid annoying these bloggers or group members.

5. Social Media Platforms

The first step in learning how to take advantage of social media is to know which platforms are worth your time and effort. In business terms, you want to profile your target audience and leverage the social media that they're most likely to be using. Like any business project, it doesn't make any sense to funnel your resources into something that won't give you a return.

The biggest names in social media right now are Facebook, Twitter, YouTube, Pinterest, LinkedIn, and Google Plus. You should get acquainted with each of them. Even if you decide that some of them aren't worth your time, you need to know enough about them to recognize which ones deserve your attention.

Facebook

Facebook was started in 2004 as a sort of interactive yearbook for college students. Students could add "friends" to build a virtual friend network, post comments on each other's "walls," and update their statuses. Since then, Facebook has steadily added new features like instant messaging, a news feed, and groups, making the site a hub for social interaction. It also opened its doors to everybody 13 and up. In 2012, Facebook surpassed 1 billion active users worldwide. That means that roughly 1 in 7 people in the world use Facebook regularly.

While Facebook began strictly for personal profiles, it expanded functionality to include business and fan pages along the way. Most large companies and celebrities now have a presence on Facebook, and many use it as one of their primary connections to fans.

Facebook also introduced the "Like," a fast and convenient way for friends and fans to express their approval of a status update, picture, video, article, etc. The Like button soon found itself beyond the confines of Facebook itself, and now many, if not most, prominent websites feature a Like button for both their home pages and their individual web pages and posts.

Aside from its ubiquity, Facebook is attractive to business owners because its business pages are nearly as flexible and fully-featured as a website. The business page is versatile enough that you can use it to post updates, upload pictures, sell products directly to customers, offer exclusive deals, and have conversations with fans. It is a great way to gauge general opinion of your products and services and respond to their questions and concerns in a public space.

Twitter

Twitter was started in 2006 as a microblogging service. Microblogging just means posting online text like a blog, but in a much smaller space. Specifically, each "microblog post" is called a tweet, expressed in 140 characters or less. Originally, tweeting was described as an SMS text message sent to a group of people. It's seen a meteoric rise in popularity—Twitter now has over 500 million active users.

The way it works is, individuals who want updates from a particular friend, business, or celebrity will "follow" them. Twitter followers can see tweets and interact with them by replying, retweeting, and clicking links contained in the tweet.

Here's an example of a tweet:

"Just found a great recipe on this cooking website [hyperlink here]!" #recipes

Notice that symbol following the short message. Unlike Facebook, Twitter was designed with something called a hashtag (traditionally called the pound sign or number sign). The "#" symbol is placed before keywords that someone might use to find the topic of a tweet. In the previous example, people who want to find recipes might search for "#recipes," find this tweet, and then click the included hyperlink to check out the website. That makes it attractive for businesses.

The other reason Twitter is great for businesses is that your tweets can go viral. If you have followers, and they think one of your tweets is worth sharing, they can "retweet" it to their own followers. That can result in your tweet becoming a "trending" topic. You can also use Twitter to offer exclusive deals or share quick tips about your industry. These things will make customers appreciate your brand.

YouTube

YouTube was started in 2005 as a video-sharing website where its users could post videos they wanted to share. It was designed as a video watching experience that caters to the individual. By searching

the site, you can now find millions of user-created and user-shared videos on every topic imaginable. Each user can create their own "channel," which mimics a television channel in that it has a specific focus and is intended for a particular audience.

Along the way, YouTube implemented a revenue-sharing model for popular user-generated content. What that means is, any individual or business with a YouTube channel that gets regular traffic can make money off of their original videos. While you shouldn't discount it as a way of earning some money, very few people can make enough money off YouTube videos to treat it as their primary means of income.

Instead, YouTube is useful as a marketing platform. You can use it to post unique, helpful videos with content that relates to your business, such as news updates, quick tips, how-to guides, and promos about your new product offerings. Like with Facebook and Twitter, it's a two-way street. You post videos, but others can post comments below the video and even post their own video responses. Treat it as another opportunity to both demonstrate your expertise and get customer feedback.

Pinterest

Pinterest was founded in 2010 as a bulletin-board style photo-sharing website, where users can "pin" photos in theme-based collections. These image collections are sort of like the analogue to YouTube channels, in that users post pictures related to a particular focus or theme. Some examples of themes might be interests, events, hobbies, and the like. Pinterest has a much smaller active user base of about 11 million, but the users are passionate and it's one of the fastest growing social networking sites.

In 2012, Pinterest implemented business pinboards. These are largely the same as pinboards for individuals, but feature distinct business profiles. Because of the ease of use and the visual nature of Pinterest, conversion rates are actually higher than those of other social media sites. This is because you're part of a rich community of people who share visual content that they think is useful or interesting. Not every business is suited to marketing through images, but anyone in art, film, graphic design, interior decorating, real estate, and similar fields might get a lot of mileage out of Pinterest.

LinkedIn

LinkedIn was founded in 2003 as a social networking site devoted to professionals. In essence, it formalized the idea of getting hired through networking by setting up an online space where people could look for jobs through their professional network of contacts. The members of your network are called "connections," and you add them similarly to how you add Facebook friends.

Every professional should have a LinkedIn profile, because it's a way to legitimize your expertise and show your credentials. LinkedIn profiles include resumes and work history, as well as listing which connections you have. Finding professional work has always been a matter of "who-you-know," and now that LinkedIn has a virtual community of connections, it's practically a necessity for staying competitive.

As for businesses, LinkedIn is a great way to stay relevant in your industry. If you do any hiring, LinkedIn is one of the best places to look for new employees. It offers a way to screen for quality prospects. Independent contractors might also find clients through LinkedIn, either through connections or through your business profile.

Google Plus

Google Plus (also written as Google +) is a social network launched in 2011. It immediately stands out from other social media sites because it's more of a "social layer" added to the broader suite of online offerings by Google. Since Google is still the most popular search engine by far, Google Plus is competitive with the other largest social media sites, and is considered a direct competitor to Facebook. It currently has 235 million active users.

Google's answer to Facebook's "Like" is the "+1." Since Google Plus is integrated with Google search, a +1 still does a lot more for a webpage's search engine ranking than a Like or a tweet. The +1 is shared with the rest of a Google Plus user's friends and contacts.

Another benefit of Google Plus for business owners is that it has the resources of Google behind it. Google has built it from the ground up to support business, with in-depth data about +1s and conversion rates. If you already use Google services, it makes sense to check out Google Plus as another way to reach your customers.

6. Building Your Network

Signing up for social media sites is the easy part. Getting the most out of them for your business takes some knowledge and persistence. No matter which one(s) you choose, however, the key is to build up your network. Generally, the more friends, fans, and followers you have, the better your business will benefit—although a network of 100,000 fair-weather friends might not beat 1000 die-hard fans, so you still have to balance quantity with quality.

Profile Design

Before you ever start trying to build a network, you have to design a profile that will attract and retain the interest of your prospects. One of the biggest mistakes businesses make is to assume that a half-hearted social media presence is better than no presence at all. As with your product offerings and your customer service, your social media profiles are a reflection on your brand. A well-designed and attractive Facebook page, YouTube channel, or other social media profile will be a positive contribution to your brand equity, while a shoddy one could drive customers away.

So, what are some considerations that will help your social media profile stand out? Well, for one thing, your design choices should be informed by what you hope to accomplish with your profile. Are you focusing on a particular topic or strategy? Make it clear at a glance what your social media profile is all about. In addition, if you have a logo or brand colors, it's a good idea to maintain consistency with your overall brand.

Another important consideration is customization. Each of your social media profiles can be customized to a great extent with backgrounds, playlists, tabs, information, images, and more. Some companies actually help businesses create customized profiles that will appeal to the target audience. Depending on how serious you are about using social media for your business, it might be worth looking into a service that helps you build unique and attractive social media profiles.

Content Plug-Ins

On many websites these days, you've probably noticed some buttons located next to an article or post: "Like," "Tweet," "+1," "Digg," "Pin It,"

"LinkedIn Share," etc. What these do is allow visitors to a site to quickly engage the social media of their choosing without ever leaving the current webpage. For example, you could be reading a fascinating news story, decide it's something others in your network should read, and use any of those buttons to share it with that respective network.

As a business owner, those buttons are your best friend. One of your primary jobs is to produce grade-A content to attract new business. When people come across your videos, articles, blog posts, pictures, or other content, they can immediately share your content with their entire network by clicking Like, Tweet, etc. It's simple to install the buttons, too. The social media companies provide code for their buttons, and you can simply copy it into your blog or website code.

These buttons are also useful because search engines don't like isolated websites. If your website is a nexus of social media interaction, that will do wonders for your search engine ranking—which, in turn, will get more people to your website to share your content with their networks. While it's a commitment to be involved with social media, the rewards can be substantial.

There's another set of buttons for your website that link to your social media profiles. You can use them to encourage people who like your content to immediately become fans on Facebook, follow you on Twitter, subscribe to your YouTube channel, and more. With these content plug-ins, you'll integrate your content with each of the various social media profiles you have—and you'll increase the benefits that come with being active on social media.

Joining Groups/Orgs/Industry Pages

Another approach to building your network is to join Facebook groups, LinkedIn industry pages, Twitter categories, etc. These are pages that are sorted by topic or function. Each works somewhat differently, but the gist is that your business's social media profile can itself be part of a larger community. For example, if you're an entrepreneur, you might join a Facebook group catering to start-ups or business owners. As part of the conversation, you can improve your visibility as a member of that industry. The same goes for comparable pages on LinkedIn and Twitter.

Prompting High Engagement

After you've achieved a good-sized network on the social media sites of your choice, you might ask what's next? As nice as it is to see the number of fans, friends, and followers growing, that doesn't automatically translate into a more successful business. Once you have attracted people to your profile, it's time to engage and interact with your audience.

Community

The best way to describe the goal of social media marketing is community. You want a community built around your products and your brand. Whether you are entertaining or informing the target audience, it needs to be worth people's time and energy to visit your profile again and again. Some campaigns are successful because they're funny or interesting or novel, while others are successful because the content is highly useful and original. Both will get people talking, and that's what you want, because people talking about your business leads to new customers.

Another important point about community is interacting with your fans and followers. As you might recall, social media is a *two-way street*, so instead of posting a status update or a tweet and going on your merry way, it's important to dedicate some time to interacting with your audience. That means responding to comments and questions, asking fans some questions, and generally making they feel heard and cared about. As a customer, if you could choose between two businesses whose products were identical, but where one actually engaged with its customers on social media, you would choose the one who interacted with its customers over the one who didn't.

Of course, timing has a lot to do with it. A community isn't going to form around a social media profile where posts are sporadic and infrequent. You should engage with your customers on a regular and predictable basis. Responding to a comment or question from four months ago defeats the purpose. As for what time of day to post new content on your profile, that depends a lot on your industry and when your target audience is likely to be online. However, a good rule of thumb is to post once in the morning, and once at the end of the workday. More important is to be consistent, so that your community can make checking your profile a part of their routine.

One more thing about community as it relates to Facebook in particular. It's possible to actually measure how successful your community is with hard data using something called "Edgerank Checking Tools." Put simply, "Edgerank" is an algorithm based on a few factors that determines how often a page will show up in Facebook users' news feeds. Since most people don't frequently check the fan pages that they've "Liked," it's important that your updates show up in your customers' news feeds. That keeps you in front of them every time they're on Facebook.

Incentives

As they say, content is king—that is, unless you're offering people *other* incentives to come back to your profile. Even if your content isn't the best there ever was, if people love your products and know that you offer discounts, coupons, sales, rewards, or giveaways on your profile, they're going to check back from time to time. That doesn't mean you should just start giving away your products and services all the time—it's merely one possible strategy for building a community.

It can go a step further than merely giving incentives for visiting the profile, though. Savvy social media marketers will give their fans and followers a reward for doing something helpful. For example, you might offer customers a discount on a product if they retweet your offer to their Twitter followers. You can get creative with the incentives you offer so that social media becomes an integral part of your marketing campaign.

Contests

An extension of the incentive idea, contests get fans even more involved in the community. Enthusiastic fans will enter a contest just because they love your brand. Mainstream companies have contests that ask fans to make a video, suggest a T-shirt design, write a jingle, make a logo, and more. There's no reason you can't leverage social media to do the same kind of promotion. The reward for a contest winner might be a discount or a gift card, of course, but often the reward is that fans get to see their creations used on your profile or in your marketing materials. When you give fans a stake in what your business is doing, you're building a community that cares.

Multimedia

In the age of Web 2.0, most social media platforms allow you to post all different kinds of media. Don't stop at text—work in images, embed videos (especially from your YouTube channel), use infographics, link to audio files like podcasts, and more. It's about cross-promotion and acknowledging the fact that some people might be persuaded to buy because of a video, but they wouldn't sit around for a podcast or read a lot of text.

7. Investing in Social Media Advertising

There are more ways to build your network besides word-of-mouth and organic growth. You can speed the process along by purchasing various kinds of online advertisements through the social media platforms of your choice. Depending on your business and the social networks you belong to, you'll probably find that certain platforms lend themselves better to different kinds of campaigns. With several social media sites and types of advertising to choose from, there's plenty of testing to be done to see which strategy pays off the best for your business.

Pay Per Click

Pay per click (PPC) advertising is a holdover from Google AdWords and other online advertising platforms. It's a pretty simple concept: an image with a short caption appears on a targeted number of people's screens, and every time someone clicks on the ad, you pay anywhere from a few cents to several dollars. More importantly, the click takes them to your website or profile, where they can take further action.
If your marketing is primarily B2B (business to business), then LinkedIn's PPC ad program will be right down your alley. If your marketing is primarily B2C (business to consumer), then Facebook is probably the best solution. On Facebook, another goal that you might have with PPC ads is simply getting more "Likes" on your business page. Since your Facebook posts are distributed to a percentage of the users who have "Liked" your page, one strategy might just be to focus on getting a lot of "Likes."

Featured Posts

One of Facebook's more recent advertising options is to pay for your posts to be featured in users' news feeds. As discussed earlier, Facebook has an Edgerank algorithm that determines how often your fans see your Facebook updates in their feed. If you want more fans and their friends to see your posts, you can pay money for the privilege. The reason this can be useful is that it's targeting people who have already "Liked" your page, or friends of theirs who are more likely to consider you because they know their friends like you. In a sense, these people are already qualified buyers. With PPC ads, you are targeting a specific demographic, but they have no previously demonstrated interest in your business or your brand. Featured posts can be worth it if you have particular goals in mind. Ideally, you should use it on posts that include a call to action, such as one that offers a discount on merchandise in your store. Otherwise, you're getting greater exposure on a post that doesn't have a likely return on your investment. You should also consider the "quality" of your fans. What that means is, if you have a bunch of fake "Likes" from people who don't really care about your business, you're still paying to have your posts appear in their news feed—which is a waste of money if they would never consider buying from you. Before you pay for any featured posts, it's a good idea to prune your "Likes" to qualified buyers—especially if you are selling a service that's confined to a specific geographical area.

Sponsored Fans

Twitter and Facebook have various ways of using word-of-mouth as a marketing strategy for businesses. It boils down to the fact that people with popular profiles can encourage their many fans or followers to check out your business. As an example, if you're an author, you might find a popular Twitter profile that talks about books, and offer to pay them to tweet an endorsement of your latest book. Rather than waiting around and hoping that a popular fan of yours spreads the word, you can take charge and pay someone to do it.

Who should you choose? Well, there are a lot of factors, but it's not dissimilar from how you would market yourself. You want to find someone who's got a sufficient number of fans or followers, and you want the target audience to be receptive to what they say. It takes some research, but it can be the very best way to reach a qualified group you've never had contact with before. As for the post a sponsored fan might write, it can be as simple as this:

"Hey guys, I just read this great new book: [link here]
You should check it out!"

8. Implementing Popular Social Media Tools

There are plenty of tools to help you implement your social media campaigns. As exciting as social media marketing is, it still represents just one small item on your business to-do list. In other words, you want all the help you can get to achieve results quickly and with as few resources expended as possible. That's where the following tools can help.

Cross-Platform Apps

If you've been feeling distressed reading about how much time social media can take, take heart: there are innovative cross-platform apps that can reduce your burden. What's a cross-platform app? It's a utility that helps you post content to multiple social media platforms at the same time! As you can imagine, that saves a tremendous amount of time if you're posting things multiple times per day, several days per week. Two of the most prominent cross-platform automation tools are Hootsuite and Tweetdeck.

There's one caveat to be aware of, though. Each social media platform caters to different audiences and has different features, so it's not always wise to approach them with a one-size-fits-all strategy. The best time to use these cross-platform apps is when making announcements that apply to anyone who's a fan or follower. For promotions, it's best to tackle each platform separately and with greater attention to detail.

Watching Analytics and Trends

Anyone versed in marketing knows that there is no such as thing as a perfect campaign. There will always be successes and disappointments, and in order to keep improving, the best thing to do is track and analyze the data related to your social media efforts. To that end, many social media sites include analytics for businesses. With the data you track, you can find out a number of very useful things. When it comes to analytics, you are looking to see things like:

- How many people are joining your network vs. leaving your network
- Which posts were liked and shared the most (and why?)
- What the demographic breakdown for your brand is
- What the conversion rate for various ads and posts is

Of all the different analytics, the conversion rate is probably the most important. It looks at how many impressions or views an ad received, how many people clicked on it, and how many people took the desired action after clicking (which usually means buying something or signing up on a subscriber list). The conversion rate helps you figure out what's working with your customers and what isn't.

Another important thing to track is consumer sentiment. The beautiful thing about social media is that people willingly say what they like and dislike about a company and its products. In addition to reading what your fans and followers are saying, you can set up Google Alerts for specific keywords like your name or the name of your business. Then, you can see what people think. This is about trends, not individuals. You want to know what most people like and dislike about your business so that you can tailor your offerings to what they're asking for. Of course, it's possible to go overboard in seeking out the feedback of strangers, but if you have dedicated followers on Facebook, Twitter, YouTube, etc., it's worth listening to what they have to say.

9. How to Turn Your Blog Post Into a Video

Nowadays, people are becoming more and more visual, preferring videos to text. Thus, you have to learn how to re-purpose your blog entry to reach the visually oriented segment of your target market. Here are some ways to do that:

Using Slides and Recording

An easy way to turn your blog post into a video is to create slides out of your article. It is an efficient way of explaining complex concepts about your brand. You can summarize the main points of your article and convert them into PowerPoint or Keynote slides. You can use the outline that you prepared for your blog entry as starting point for your slides.

You can even record a voice over narration about your blog entry in your slides. PowerPoint and Keynote are two of the easiest software to use if you want to create slides that can be converted to videos. They allow you to record voice over narration and use other features and effects to make your video more interesting.

You On Cam Talking About It

If you are confident to face the camera, you can also create your own video with you as talent. You can even create a video blog or a vlog to showcase your videos.

Avoid simply reading your blog entry in front of the camera. Your followers might be bored if they realize that you are just reading off your blog. They might lose interest if they see that you are not really offering them anything new.

You may want to summarize what you said in your article and give your thoughts on the topic. You can work on the comments that you received about the blog entry in your social networking accounts or answer frequently asked questions. You can also create how to videos or show expert interviews about your blog entry.

As you go along the way, think of other creative ways to present your blog entry through videos.

Animation

Admittedly, however, not all of us are confident to face the camera. Fortunately, technology now allows you to create something interesting out of your blog post without subjecting you to excessive embarrassment.

One option you can explore is the creation of animation. There are a number of available free online software that you can use to create animations such as goanimate.com. Of course, a free subscription would mean limited features. These sites do everything for you. You just need to pick the setting and characters that suit your brand and type the text of the narration or dialogue that you want and your animation will be ready for sharing and viewing.

You can also use animated GIFs to create interesting videos out of your blog post. A GIF is a series of still photos coded into a single file. It is a means of bringing your otherwise still photographs to life. You often see it on online memes.

The nice thing about GIFs is they allow you to zoom in on the most important part or message of your animation, making it easier for you to connect to your clients.

10. Where to Share Your Video for Maximum Exposure

Similar to your blog post, your video will be worthless if you do not share them with others. Sharing your video is not as simple as putting it online. You should learn how to distribute it in such a way that will ensure maximum exposure. Here are some sites that you can use:

YouTube

Of course, when it comes to video sharing, YouTube is still your best bet. Here are some reasons why:

•   It has been there for a long time.
•   It is and it will continue to be popular, with billions of users.
•   It is free.
•   Depending on the settings you choose for your video, your content can be available to anyone on the Internet, thereby increasing your brand's online presence.
•   The more views you get, the more leads and potential customers your business will have.
•   It is easy to use.
•   It is easy to share your video through HTML coding. It also has share buttons to make it easy for you to send your video to your e-mail and Facebook contacts.
•   You can add annotations to your video, containing clickable calls to action. You can put links to your website or other marketing materials on the top part of the video.
•   You can adjust the look of your YouTube channel to mirror your brand to further promote your business. For your layout, choose Player View so you can set your video to auto play. Take advantage of the Playlists feature by including your most popular videos there.

Just like any other social media tool out there, there are also some disadvantages to using YouTube, such as the following:

- Since the site is accessible to anyone online, it is quite difficult to filter the authentic videos from the spam ones. Comments can also be irrelevant and rude due to limited regulation.
- It is a public venue so be ready to be exposed to the public as well. Do not be surprised if you get stalkers in the process.
- It might be difficult to stand out because there are just too many videos out there. You need to optimize your video to get continuous views, which can take up a lot of your time. To make your video more searchable, you should use targeted keywords in your title, description, and tags.
- If you do not follow the required YouTube specifications, your video can be shrunk to meet the requirements, thereby sacrificing its quality.

Like all other video sharing sites, your video's content greatly matters. Make sure to create compelling videos that appeal to what your target market needs.

Vimeo

Vimeo is the place for video sharing for professionals who are interested in high quality and creative video content. Some advantages to using Vimeo are as follows:

- You get better, relevant, and more constructive comments as the viewers are more engaged.
- Viewers can focus more on your video because its layout is minimalist, doing away with the advertisements and comments that pop up on YouTube.
- Video quality is often better for Vimeo uploaded files.

Here are some of its disadvantages:

- It gets fewer visitors than YouTube.
- You cannot upload content that you did not fully create by yourself.
- If you want promote a product or service, you are required to subscribe to its paid Pro account.

•	It has cap restrictions for uploading, even for its Pro accounts.

Dailymotion

Dailymotion is another video sharing site that you can use. Some of its advantages include:

•	It is not too strict on copyright matters because producers are not that attentive to this site.
•	Although it has fewer viewers and it may not be as popular as the other sites, it also offers an HD option.

However, here are some of its disadvantages:

•	It is still a small player compared to YouTube and Vimeo.
•	Videos uploaded here should not exceed 150 MB and 20 minutes.

11. How to Turn Your Blog Post to Audio

Now that you have successfully turned and distributed your blog post into a video, it is time to explore other means of re-purposing your blog content. One way to do it is by converting your blog post to audio.

Like videos, audio versions of your blog entry are also interesting and unique ways of conveying your message to your target market. Audio podcasts for instance reach more customers and can attract even more potential clients for your brand. They can be easily downloaded to MP3 players, iPods, or even smart phones, and the listeners can access them anytime and anywhere they want.

Using Audacity and Other Audio Programs

To convert your blog post into an audio podcast, you just need to find a website that provides text-to-speech service that can read the text contained in your RSS feeds and convert it into a computer-generated speech. You can try creating accounts with sites like Odiogo and iSpeech. The software should provide a text-to-speech plug-in for your blog on its site. Once you have installed and activated the plug-in in your blog, it should appear there and you should be able to test it when you click the Listen or Play button.

Audacity is one software that you can also use for this purpose. It is a free open source digital audio recording and editor software application. It works on multiple platforms like Linux, Mac, Windows, and other operating systems. Its features include the following:

* Recording and playing back audio from multiple sources;
* Importing and exporting different file formats supported by libsndfile library like WAV and MP3;

• Post-processing of different types of audio like podcasts by adding effects like fading in and out, trimming, and normalization; and
• Recording and mixing entire albums.

Its free and open nature has made Audacity popular with its easy and flexible user interface.

Extracting Audio from the Video You Created

Apart from converting your blog entry into an audio file, you can also extract the audio from the video you created and distribute the same to different platforms. Here are some free online tools that you can use to do that:

• Oxelon Media Converter. It has a direct stream copy feature that allows you to rip high quality audio from video files like AVI.
• Pazera Audio Extractor. This only works on Windows but it can extract audio from different file formats. Output will be in WAV, AAC, MP3, and WMA formats, among others. It has pre-defined settings and it is easy to use.
• Any Audio Converter. This is also limited to Windows. It can extract audio from different video formats and from DVDs.
• Audacity. The nice thing about this software is it works across different platforms like Mac, Linux, and Windows. Although the tool is more advanced compared to the other software, its easy to use interface makes it a preferred choice of many.
• AoA Audio Extractor. It can extract audio from video files, including flash files like FLV. It can also rip just specific parts of the track and not the entire audio.
• VidtoMP3. It can convert audio from videos taken from sites like Vimeo, YouTube, and Megavideo. The output is an MP3 file that can be downloaded.
• iExtractMP3. This is an ideal software for Mac users. It can rip audio from video files like FLV, without sacrificing its quality.
• Free Audio Editor. Apart from extracting audio from video files, it can also download YouTube videos. It supports noise reduction and audio recording.

- YouTube to MP3 Mozilla Firefox Add-on. Firefox users can download YouTube videos as MP3 files by using this add-on. It also works on other sites like Dailymotion.
- VLC. While more known as a video player, it can also remove video content from the input source and convert the audio to your desired format.

12. Audio Distrubution Platforms

Now that you have valuable audio files in your possession, it is time to find reliable media where you can distribute them for maximum exposure. Here are some tools that you can use for spreading your podcasts or audio files:

iTunes

iTunes is a media player and library application created by Apple. Because many people use it and Apple products have this exclusive feel to them, people have the impression that you are with the big leagues already if you are on iTunes. You also reach a wider audience if you use this software.

Your program and new episodes will be automatically downloaded to the iTunes program folder of your subscribers. The subscriber can access your podcast through his Apple devices anytime and anywhere.

Uploading your podcast to iTunes is free and it's easy. Make sure though that your podcast meets the specifications required by iTunes, otherwise, your podcast might not work properly and it might not be effective in reaching your target market.

Note that the iTunes team reviews each submission before it can be published. It may take a week or two before your podcast can be approved.

Spreaker

Spreaker is an online social networking community for musicians, producers, and broadcasters. You can directly upload your podcast or your can record it through DJ Console. All shows are listed in its directory, making it easier to find good shows and to connect with other members.

It offers both paid and free services. A free subscription allows 10 hours of storage, with recordings limited to 30 minutes. The pricing plan for the paid subscription depends on the number of hours of audio that you have stored with Spreaker and the length of each recording you can upload. Its features also include providing advanced analytics and adding custom intro commercials.

Spreaker is a reliable and reasonably priced service provider that also syndicates to other platforms like Zune and iTunes.

SoundCloud

SoundCloud is an online social networking community for musicians. While geared more towards uploading songs, it also allows uploading of podcasts.

It offers statistics to its members and you can get your own audio page for your podcasts. It also has a dedicated application for iPad.

SoundCloud offers a free 14-day trial for you to test its service. Afterwards, you can subscribe to their paid plans, which are priced reasonably. Each plan has corresponding restrictions with regard to the length of audio that can be uploaded.

Podcasting Directories

Apart from the platforms mentioned above, you can also distribute your podcasts through various podcasting directories like the following:

- **TalkShoe.** It is a free java-based radio and podcasting service that allows you to participate in radio shows which can be syndicated as podcasts. A host facilitates the show and up to 250 people can participate through VOIP, Skype, or its own software called ShoePhone. It does not restrict the number of recording hours and it even allows you to upload older episodes of your podcast.
- **Libsyn.** It is a well-known podcast hosting service used by popular podcasters. You get your own page and smart phone app. Profits from app sales are equally shared with Libsyn. It also offers iTunes compatibility and detailed statistics of downloads. Plan prices vary depending on the size of files you can upload per month. It also boasts of a user-friendly interface.

Hipcast. It offers you an iPhone app, directory listing, and iTunes syndication. You can record your podcast by calling a special phone number designated by **Hipcast.** You get a 7-day free trial before subscribing to the paid plans. Its plans are reasonably priced and you get increased storage every month.

13. How to Turn Your Blog Post into Images

Another way to re-purpose your blog post is to turn it into interesting and appealing images. This will give your inbound marketing strategy a colorful and lively aspect. This will also help you connect with your readers who are more visually oriented.

Here are some tools that you can use to turn your blog entry into images:

Infographics (Show Infographic Programs)

Infographics, or information graphics, are popular means for presenting complex data, knowledge, or information quickly and clearly through graphic visual representations. Think of it as your modern day graph or flow chart. Infographics are very handy especially if there are complex details about your brand that you want to explain to your followers. Just make sure that you come up with well-designed infographics so you can maximize their potential.

Here are some reasons why infographics will be good for your business:

•   Studies show that 90% of the information we remember is based on visual impact. People also have shorter attention span nowadays and are more used to simply scanning text without really reading them. Thus, infographics are simple visual aids that will make your brand stand out.
•   They are more eye-catching than plain text since you can use different colors, content, movement, and images to get your readers' attention. They allow you to provide informative and educational materials about your brand and to entertain your followers at the same time.
•   Sharing them online is fairly easy. Some blogs or websites provide you with an embed code for the infographic you published,

allowing an automatic link from the original site to your own site. You can easily share infographics through your social networking accounts and because they look more appealing, there's a bigger chance of your infographics going viral. Hopefully, this can generate interesting comments from your followers.

•   When your infographics go viral, receiving a lot of likes, clicks, or shares, this will help your website's ranking in the Google algorithm. Of course, this will be good for your SEO campaign.

•   They are good tools for reinforcing your brand. You can incorporate your company's logo, message, colors, shapes, and over-all look to your infographics to help increase awareness about your brand.

Here are some things to consider when making good infographics:

•   Make sure they are based on good and reliable data. Your sources should be worth reading to begin with and your data should be updated.

•   Create a mini-story to keep your followers engaged – have a beginning, a climax, and an end.

•   Be creative without looking tacky. Incorporate your brand so your followers can identify with your infographics.

•   Avoid overcrowding your infographics. Highlight the important parts and minimize use of text to make them easier to read.

Using Quotes/Steps from Your Post

If you do not have the time or the skills to create infographics, you can still turn your blog posts into images.

Look for interesting quotable quotes from your blog post and turn this into an image and share it through your social networking accounts. There are a number of websites that can convert your quotes into beautiful images such as the following:

•   Behappy.me
•   Inspirably.com
•   QuotesCover.com

- Quozio.com

If there are how to or step by step guides or procedures in your blog post such as how to sign up for your website, you can turn these into an image such as a flow chart to make them easier for your readers to follow.

Using Stock Images and Adding Text, Etc. in picmonkey.com

You may have images on file that you want to share with your followers. However, you might be apprehensive that the image alone looks boring or bland. You might want to embellish your images a bit to make them more appealing.

There are a number of options online that allow you to edit your images for free. One of these sits is picmonkey.com. Here are some of its interesting features:

- It's free and you don't have to register or download any software to use it.
- It's very easy to use.
- It has the standard features of other photo editors – resizing, cropping, adjusting exposure, and adding frames, effects, stickers, texts, overlays, logos, and watermarks.
- You can incorporate your quotable quotes to send out a stronger message about your brand.
- It allows you to use your own logo and other elements about your brand that will raise awareness about your business.

14. Where to Distribute Your Images

To maximize the potentials of the beautiful images that you have created, you now need to find good venues where you can share them. Here are some tools that you can utilize:

Social Media

Your social media accounts are still the best place for you to promote your images. Here are some popular sites for image sharing:

Pinterest

Pinterest is an online pin board for images and videos you want to keep in your personal and categorized collections. These images could be anything that interests you like a home design or a peg for your dream wedding. But this platform can also cater to your inbound marketing needs. Your pins will be shown on your feed and they will be visible to your followers.

Here are some of its features:

- You can provide your pins with relevant keywords and a summary to make them easier to find.
- Other people can re-pin your pins to share them with their own followers. People can comment on your pins, making Pinterest a good SEO tool to drive traffic and promote personal interest to your brand.

- Options to personalize your page are limited, unlike other social media sites.
- You can share your pins in your Facebook and Twitter accounts by integrating your profile to these sites.

Instagram

Instagram is a popular online photo-sharing site. Here are some of its features:

- It allows you to take pictures and record 15-second videos that you can upload to your Instagram account and share in your other social networking accounts like Facebook and Twitter.
- It offers several digital filters that you can apply to your images.
- It has millions of members so the images you share will reach a lot of people.
- Photos are confined to a square shape, different from the usual 16:9 ratio used by mobile cameras.

The Usual Suspects – Facebook and Twitter

Do not ignore your trusted social networking accounts on Facebook and Twitter as they will most probably still have more followers than your other social media accounts. So while you use them for sharing status updates, blog links, videos, and a host of other stuff, make sure to utilize them as well for sharing your images. You will definitely benefit from all the comments, likes, shares, and retweets that your images will get.

Image Sites

You can also use image sites to post the images you have created. While some of these sites appear like social media, they focus more on the image itself, thereby putting them in a different category. Here are some sites you can consider:

Flickr

This is a community for photo sharing that has the following features:

- It allows you to store and share your own photos.
- Other users can view and comment on your photos.
- You can organize and arrange your photos into galleries and sets.
- You can adjust the privacy and other settings of your photos.
- You need to sign up for a paid pro account to have unlimited video and photo uploads.

500px

500px is a more exclusive image site compared to Flickr. It is a repository of really good photographs shared by great and passionate photographers. Other users can give feedback on your photos and you can expect to receive more serious comments here. You also need to subscribe to a paid account if you want to get unlimited uploads and use your personal domain name with the site.

Picasa Web Albums

Picasa is Google's free image organizer and viewer that also allows photo sharing. You can organize and edit your digital photos through this site. It has file tracking and importing features together with tags, collections, and facial recognition functions that help you sort your photos. It has basic photo editing functions and it allows you to e-mail or print your images.

Tumblr

Tumblr is a micro-blogging site similar to Twitter but it relies heavily on videos and images. Here are some of its features:

- Other users can re-blog, like, and comment on your posts. This is a good way of finding people who are interested in the images you share and is a useful SEO tool for your brand.
- It allows tagging and keyword searches to make your images easier to find.
- You can personalize your page depending on your preferences with the unique layouts offered by Tumblr and from other free websites.
- You can upload different types of media like images, links, audio, text, quotes, and videos.

15. Conclusion

As illustrated through the different chapters of this book, becoming a content marketing ninja is very easy. You just need to devote less than one hour per day for 14 days to master the art of inbound or content marketing to ensure that your brand will be seen everywhere. To reiterate, simply follow these easy steps and you will be well on your way to becoming a content marketing ninja:

- Write an informative and valuable blog post that will be appealing to your target market.
- Share your blog post for maximum exposure.
- Convert your blog post into a video that your clients will find entertaining.
- Share your videos through different video sharing sites.
- Turn your blog post into audio files.
- Share your audio files through different audio program sites to maximize their potential.
- Convert your blog post into lively images that will entice your followers to know more about your brand.
- Distribute your images in different image-sharing sites for maximum exposure.
- Share your status updates in your different social networking accounts and schedule when they will be posted.

Go take action!

So what are you waiting for? Spend the next days mastering the things you have learned in this book so you can be the best

internet marketer out there and expect to see great results for your brand and business.